37 Fermented Ve

A flavorful guide to krauts, ki
vegetables that taste better than pickled foods.

Your Free Gift

I want to thank you for being so awesome and buying this book.

To show my appreciation, I've put together a free gift for you:

Chutney Recipes:

http://www.stukkiesoftware.com/37-fermented-vegetable-recipes/

Just visit the link above to download your free gift.

I know you will love these recipes!

Thank you!

Jennifer Connor

Table of Contents

Your Free Gift	1
Introduction	5
Why Should You Try to Ferment Vegetables?	5
Fermenting is simple	5
Fermenting is healthy	5
Fermentation naturally preserves foods	6
How to Use This Book	6
Basic Fermentation Guide	8
Equipment Needed	8
Before Fermentation	10
During Fermentation	11
After Fermentation	11
Recipes for Different Fermentation Methods	13
Without a culture package	14
With a culture package	16
Sauerkraut	19
Classic Sauerkraut	20
Salt-Free Sauerkraut	22
Jalapeno Garlic Sauerkraut	24
Cranberry Sauerkraut	26
Cortido	28
Kimchi	31
Spicy Traditional Kimchi	32
Apple & Kale Kimchi	34
Radish & Cabbage Kimchi	36

Hot Radish Kimchi	38
Quick Kimchi	40
Individual Vegetables	43
Fermented Carrot Sticks	44
Fermented Ginger Carrots	46
Fermented Radishes	48
Fermented Spinach	50
Spicy Fermented Spinach	52
Fermented Eggplant	54
Fermented Sweet Potatoes	56
Fermented Beets	59
Fermented Cucumbers	60
Fermented Spicy Radish Spears	62
Fermented Green Beans	64
Curried Fermented Cauliflower	66
Fermented Dill Cauliflower	68
Polish Fermented Mushrooms	70
Fermented Turnips	72
Fermented Sweet Potatoes	75
Fermented Cherry Tomatoes	76
Fermented Green Cherry Tomatoes	78
Fermented Horseradish Root	80
Mixed Vegetables	83
Fermented Cauliflower, Carrots, & Peppers	84
Fermented Cauliflower, Carrots, and Garlic	86
Fermented Beets and Turnips	88

Fermented Green Beans & Carrots	90
Fermented Green Beans & Mushrooms	92
So, how did it go?	95
More Delicious Books By Jennifer Connor	96

Introduction

Fermented vegetables are the perfect snack. They are delicious and jammed packed with nutrients. Not only does the fermentation process preserve all the natural vitamins and minerals in vegetables, but fermentation also creates microbes that are great for you and your health.

You can forget about the "empty calories" you get from snacking on crackers and chips. Even pickled foods are overly processed and less beneficial to your health.

With fermented veggies, you will culture the natural nutrients in foods by just adding salt under the right conditions. With fermented veggies, you will be gaining nutrients with each tasty bite.

Why Should You Try to Ferment Vegetables?

It is simple. Fermenting vegetables is delicious, healthy, inexpensive, easy, and hard to mess up!

Fermenting is simple
Let's start with the ease. Technically, vegetables can be fermented with nothing more than salt and minimal equipment. You can vary fermentation time, temperature, and ratio with little risk in "messing it up". This means you'll feel like a professional fermenter in no time!

Fermenting is healthy
Did you know that fermentation creates microbes? These bacteria are not as scary as they sound. If fact, they aren't scary at all because they are *helpful* bacteria!

In fact, the bacteria created through the fermentation process have many health benefits including:

-Aid in digestion
-Preserves and enhances vitamins and minerals in vegetables
-Supports the immune system

Fermentation naturally preserves foods

Remember those helpful microbes we discussed? Well, those microbes allow for a natural preservation of your food. Your fermented vegetables can last for months!

Have you heard that pickling, freezing and canning vegetables diminishes the vitamins and minerals in foods? Unfortunately, that is true. But, fermenting vegetables preserves all that is good about your veggies by maintaining the great amount of vitamins and minerals. In fact, fermenting vegetables can *increase* those levels, making it even healthier than juiced or raw veggies!

Let's not forget the most important part - the taste! Ease of preparation and health benefits is not enough, you have to want to eat them! Thankfully, this guide will help you make delicious veggies that you will crave. You will discover new flavors that you will love to eat as snacks, on salads, and at meals!

The real question is, why wouldn't you want to try fermenting vegetables?

How to Use This Book

Throughout this book, you'll find a basic guide to fermenting vegetables and obviously a recipe or two!

Where to start? Well, the best way, in my humble opinion, is to look through the Basic Fermentation Guide below. This will give you an idea of what equipment you will need and what process you will take.

Then, it's time for the fun part - fermenting!

After experimenting with some of the recipes, you will begin to gain a deeper understanding of the fermentation process. Eventually, fermenting vegetables will become something that you do effortlessly. You will get to enjoy a great deal of benefits with each batch you make. Much more than those overly processed pickled foods you buy from your grocery store!

Basic Fermentation Guide

Now it is time for you to see just how simple fermenting vegetables can be. After reading through these simple techniques and suggestions, you'll be on your way to becoming a fermentation professional!

Equipment Needed

Remember, fermentation has been used for ages. So, no fancy equipment is needed. For recipes such as sauerkraut or kimchi, a food processor can be helpful. However, equipment requirements are so basic that electricity is not even required!

Fermentation Containers
Aside from vegetables and salt, you need 1 thing: a container to ferment in.

Some materials, like metals and soft plastic, are more reactive. This means that the bacteria cultures will be affected by these materials. They also may lead to materials like chrome or nickel leaching into your food! Gross.

The materials to avoid includes aluminum, copper, cast-iron, and low-grade stainless steel.

So, you only want to ferment in the following materials:
-Glass Jars
-Stoneware (ceramic)
-Silicone
-Hard (food-grade) Plastic
-High Quality Stainless-Steel

Lids

Another decision to be made is the lid you would like to use. There are 3 common preferences: cloth, air-tight, air-lock.

- Cloth: an old-aged way to ferment. This is less maintenance because the cloth allows the carbon dioxide to escape. However, it also allows oxygen in (and possible bacteria), so cloth is not the best option.

-Air-tight: the simplest option because you do not have to purchase air-locking equipment. An airtight lid will prevent oxygen and bacteria from entering. However, you will need to crack the lid daily to allow the carbon dioxide to escape.

-Air-lock lid: the lowest maintenance but often more expensive. You will need a special fermentation vessel that has this feature. The benefit is that you will not need to tend to your ferment during the fermentation time.

Temperature & Light

It is best to ferment in a dark room at temperatures between 55-75°F. That is because the "good" bacteria grow best in these conditions. It is good to ferment in a dark room of your basement because it is typically cooler. Serious fermenters may get a second refrigerator that can be kept at this temperature.

Oxygen & Carbon Dioxide

It is important that your veggies do not get exposed to oxygen. Periodically pressing down your vegetables so they don't rise above the liquid is helpful. To simplify this process, you may choose to use a fermentation weight to keep your vegetables under the brine. You can also add fresh brine on occasion to ensure your veggies are covered.

Pressing down your vegetables will also press out the carbon dioxide that forms during the fermentation process. It is important that you allow the carbon dioxide bubbles to "escape" from the brine prevent oxygen from moving in.

Fermentation Time

There is no exact "formula" to determine the right time for every batch you ferment. The vegetable, bacteria, elevation, even the season can affect time.

Thankfully, this process is hard to mess up. Remember?

So play around with timing to find what tastes best for you. Many people like their ferment to age longer like a fine wine. Others prefer to eat their veggies sooner rather than later.

Most will take a minimum of 3-6 days. Sauerkraut takes close to 6 days, other vegetables take less time.

The great news is that your fermented vegetables are safe to eat at any stage of the process. So, taste it periodically to see when it has reached a taste that you enjoy!

Before Fermentation

Wash, wash, wash!

Remember those microbes that we make during the fermentation process? Well, unfortunately, there are microbes (bacteria) on your vegetables when you buy them at the store. These aren't good like the ones we produce during fermentation. In fact, these are bad. They can make you sick and if you don't wash them off they can multiply during fermentation.

So wash your veggies, thoroughly! Then, store in a cold place until use to prevent microbes from growing.

You will also want to wash your equipment. Use hot water and soap to kill any bacteria that may linger.

Next, you will need to chop your vegetables. If you are making a sauerkraut or kimchi, you will want to shred the vegetables and a food processor can be helpful. For other vegetables, chop them to your desired size.

During Fermentation

Check your ferment periodically during the fermentation time. As long as all is going well, It will expanded and bubble.

Push down the vegetables if they come up above the water. If mold appears on the top, scrape it off as soon as possible to prevent further spoiling (the fermentation will prevent a small amount of mold from being a problem).

Pushing down the vegetables will also help the carbon dioxide escape. As previously mentioned, this is a good thing! One method is to place a fermentation weight or a cleaned plate on top of their veggies to keep everything packed down tightly.

After Fermentation

After fermented, place in the refrigerator. The fermentation process will continue, slowly, and your vegetables will age like wine. The veggies will last for at least a few months (if you don't eat them sooner!).

Recipes for Different Fermentation Methods

In this book we focus on two main ways to ferment vegetables: with a culture starter and without a culture starter. While most of the recipes in this book involve only vegetables, salt (and maybe water), you can use the recipe with a culture package as a guide for adjusting a recipe if you desire.

Without a culture package

This is the true way to ferment vegetables: just veggies and salt! Although it takes a bit longer to ferment, this is they way to go if your are looking for a traditional fermented vegetable!

Yields: 2 quarts (½ gallon)

Ingredients:

5 pounds cabbage OR about a vegetable of your choice
2 to 3 tbsp sea salt
filtered water

Directions:

Chop cabbage or vegetables to your desired size: if making sauerkraut, you may want to use a food processor. If making a different veggie, you may want bite-sized pieces.

Mix everything (except water) in a large bowl. Pound with a wooden spoon or cabbage crusher to release juices. Let sit for 5 minutes. Then pound again. These juices will replace water for a traditional fermentation.

Pack mixture into a 2 clean, quart jars. Weigh down vegetables so they are submerged in the brine with a fermentation weight or a plate that is just the right size. If there is not enough brine from the vegetable juices, add filtered water until is is 1-2 inches over vegetables.

Seal with an air-lock lid or an airtight lid. Air-tight lid will need to be cracked open daily to allow the carbon dioxide to escape.

Set in a cool, dark place for 3-6 days. Sauerkraut takes close to 6 days, other vegetables take less time.

It will expanded and bubble. Periodically check it. Push down the vegetables if they come up above the water. If mold appears on the top, scrape it off as soon as possible to prevent further spoiling (the fermentation will prevent a small amount of mold from being a problem).

After fermented, place in the refrigerator. The fermentation process will continue, slowly, and your vegetables will age like wine. The veggies will last for at least 8 months.

With a culture package

If you want to ferment a bit faster, you can try this method. A culture package also helps ensure your are getting the *right* bacteria… many believe that a culture package can result in for helpful bacteria for your body.

Yields: 2 quarts (½ gallon)

Ingredients:

5 pounds vegetables of your choice
2 to 3 tbsp Celtic sea salt
1 tsp sugar (fruit juice will work as well)
filtered water
1 package starter culture

Directions:

In a large bowl add starter culture to water and sugar to activate.

Chop cabbage or vegetables to your desired size: if making sauerkraut, you may want to use a food processor. If making a different veggie, you may want bite-sized pieces.

Mix everything (except water) in the large bowl. Pound with a wooden spoon or cabbage crusher to release juices. Let sit for 5 minutes. Then pound again. These juices will replace water for a traditional fermentation.

Pack mixture into a 2, clean, quart jars. Weigh down vegetables so they are submerged in the brine with a fermentation weight or a plate that is just the right size. If there is not enough brine from the vegetable juices, add filtered water until is is 1-2 inches over vegetables.

Seal with an air-lock lid or an airtight lid. Air-tight lid will need to be cracked open daily to allow the carbon dioxide to escape.

Set in a cool, dark place for 3-6 days. Sauerkraut takes close to 6 days, other vegetables take less time.

It will expanded and bubble. Periodically check it. Push down the vegetables if they come up above the water. If mold appears on the top, scrape it off as soon as possible to prevent further spoiling (the fermentation will prevent a small amount of mold from being a problem).

After fermented, place in the refrigerator. The fermentation process will continue, slowly, and your vegetables will age like wine. The veggies will last for at least 8 months.

Sauerkraut

If you're going to ferment vegetables, than sauerkraut is a great place to start! Enjoy these recipes with your favorite Polish Sausage, or eat it with a spoon! Either way, you'll love these different recipes!

To increase your understanding of making sauerkraut, it is helpful to know that most krauts include 2 major vegetables:

-shredded or chopped cabbage
-shredded hard root vegetables such as beets, carrot, daikon, sweet potatoes, etc.

The recipes to follow will give you some fun ideas on how to make delicious sauerkraut!

Classic Sauerkraut

Let's enjoy a classic sauerkraut which keeps you and your digestive system healthy.

Yields:1 quart

Ingredients:

1 medium head of red cabbage, about 3 pounds
2 tsp caraway seed
2 tsp sea salt
filtered water

Directions:

Chop or shred cabbage. Mix everything (except water) in a large bowl. Pound with a wooden spoon or cabbage crusher to release juices. Let sit for 5 minutes. Then pound again. These juices will replace water for a traditional fermentation.

Pack mixture into a clean, quart jar. Weigh down vegetables so they are submerged in the brine with a fermentation weight or a plate that is just the right size. If there is not enough brine from the vegetable juices, add filtered water until is is 1-2 inches over vegetables.

Seal with an air-lock lid or an airtight lid. Air-tight lid will need to be cracked open daily to allow the carbon dioxide to escape.

Set in a cool, dark place for 3-6 days.

It will expanded and bubble. Periodically check it. Push down the vegetables if they come up above the water. If mold appears on the top, scrape it off as soon as possible to prevent further spoiling (the fermentation will prevent a small amount of mold from being a problem).

Taste periodically to see if it is ready.

Once it has reached a desired flavor, place in the refrigerator. The fermentation process will continue, slowly, and your kraut will age like wine. Store up to 8 months!

Salt-Free Sauerkraut

Okay, I'll be honest, salt-free is not the best way to ferment. In fact, it's not truly "fermenting". It is less reliable and you may end up with something you need to throw away.

On the other hand, a salt-free sauerkraut which will not only enable your low sodium diet but give you delicious taste too! So, give it a try… but don't hesitate to start over if it seems to go bad.

Yields: 2 quarts (½ gallon)
Fermentation Time: 5 days

Ingredients:

2 medium heads of cabbage, about 5 pounds
1 tablespoon caraway seeds
1 tablespoon dill seeds
1 tablespoon celery seeds
1 tablespoon crushed peppercorns
filtered water

Directions:

Chop or shred cabbage. Grind seeds and peppercorns. Mix everything (except water) in a large bowl. Pound with a wooden spoon or cabbage crusher to release juices.

Pack mixture into 2 clean, quart jars. Cover with water. Leave 2-3 inches for vegetables to expand. Weigh down vegetables so they are submerged in the brine with a fermentation weight or a plate that is just the right size.

Seal with an air-lock lid or an airtight lid. Air-tight lid will need to be cracked open daily to allow the carbon dioxide to escape.

Set in a cool, dark place for 5-8 days. Taste it daily starting on day 5 to see when it is ready.

It will expanded and bubble. Periodically check it. Push down the vegetables if they come up above the water. If mold appears on the top, scrape it off as soon as possible to prevent further spoiling (the fermentation will prevent a small amount of mold from being a problem). Since you aren't using salt, check the smell. If it smells sour, throw it away and try again.

Once it has reached a desired flavor, place in the refrigerator. The fermentation process will continue, slowly, and your kraut will age like wine.

Jalapeno Garlic Sauerkraut

This is a spicy recipe really mixes up your usual kraut experience! Plus… the red cabbage makes is hot pink!

Yields: 1 quart
Fermentation Time: 3 weeks

Ingredients:

1 medium head of red cabbage, about 3 pounds (shredded)
3 cloves garlic (minced)
4 medium jalapeno peppers (sliced thin)
1 tablespoon unrefined sea salt
filtered water

Directions:

Chop or shred vegetables. Mix everything (except water) in a large bowl. Pound with a wooden spoon or cabbage crusher to release juices. Let sit for 5 minutes. Then pound again. These juices will replace water for a traditional fermentation.

Pack mixture into a clean, quart jar. Weigh down vegetables so they are submerged in the brine with a fermentation weight or a plate that is just the right size. If there is not enough brine from the vegetable juices, add filtered water until is is 1-2 inches over vegetables.

Seal with an air-lock lid or an airtight lid. Air-tight lid will need to be cracked open daily to allow the carbon dioxide to escape.

Set in a cool, dark place for about 1 week.

It will expanded and bubble. Periodically check it. Push down the vegetables if they come up above the water. If mold appears on the top, scrape it off as soon as possible to prevent further spoiling (the fermentation will prevent a small amount of mold from being a problem).

Taste it around 1 week to see when it is ready.

Once it has reached a desired flavor, place in the refrigerator. The fermentation process will continue, slowly, and your kraut will age like wine. Store up to 8 months!

Cranberry Sauerkraut

A fun treat during the holidays! Your family will love this kraut.

Yields: 2 quarts

Ingredients:

1 head of cabbage (about 3 pounds), shredded
1 cup shredded carrots
½ tsp bay leaves, grinded
2 tbsp sugar
1 cup cranberries
1 liter filtered water

Directions:

Shred cabbage and carrots. Mix in a large bowl. Pound with a wooden spoon or cabbage crusher to release juices. Let sit for 5 minutes. Then pound again to get maximum juices.

In a pot, boil water. Add salt, sugar and bay leaves. Remove from heat and pour over cabbage mixture.

Pack mixture into a clean, quart jar. Weigh down vegetables so they are submerged in the brine with a fermentation weight or a plate that is just the right size. If there is not enough brine, add filtered water until it is 1-2 inches over vegetables.

Seal with an air-lock lid or an airtight lid. Air-tight lid will need to be cracked open daily to allow the carbon dioxide to escape.

Set in a cool, dark place for about 1 week.

It will expanded and bubble. Periodically check it. Push down the vegetables if they come up above the water. If mold appears on the top, scrape it off as soon as possible to prevent further spoiling (the fermentation will prevent a small amount of mold from being a problem).

Taste it around 1 week to see when it is ready. When you approve of the taste, add cranberries to jar and mix.

Store in the refrigerator. The fermentation process will continue, slowly, and your kraut will age like wine. Store up to 8 months!

Cortido

A Latin American Style sauerkraut. These flavors make for a delicious twist on your traditional kraut.

Yields: 2 quarts

Ingredients:

1 large cabbage, cored and shredded
1 cup carrots, grated
2 medium onions, quartered lengthwise and very finely sliced
1 tablespoon dried oregano
¼ – ½ teaspoon red pepper flakes
2 tablespoons sea salt

Directions:

Shred cabbage and carrots. Mix in a large bowl. Pound with a wooden spoon or cabbage crusher to release juices. Let sit for 5 minutes. Then pound again to get maximum juices.

Pack cabbage and all other ingredients into jar. Weigh down vegetables so they are submerged in the brine with a fermentation weight or a plate that is just the right size. If there is not enough brine, add filtered water until it is 1-2 inches over vegetables.

Seal with an air-lock lid or an airtight lid. Air-tight lid will need to be cracked open daily to allow the carbon dioxide to escape.

Set in a cool, dark place for about 1 week.

It will expanded and bubble. Periodically check it. Push down the vegetables if they come up above the water. If mold appears on the top, scrape it off as soon as possible to prevent further spoiling (the fermentation will prevent a small amount of mold from being a problem).

Taste it around 1 week to see when it is ready. When you approve of the taste, add cranberries to jar and mix.

Store in the refrigerator. The fermentation process will continue, slowly, and your kraut will age like wine. Store up to 8 months!

Kimchi

A Korean tradition that tastes super delicious!

Kimchi is similar to sauerkraut except that it is spicer and the cabbage is cut into larger chunks. Kimchi more commonly uses Napa Cabbage, which is traditionally grown in Asia. It often ages longer, so letting your kimchi ferment for longer periods will result in a more traditional, Kimchi flavor.

Enjoy these recipes as you explore the great flavors Kimchi can unlock!

Spicy Traditional Kimchi

If you love to have your kimchi with a traditional spicy flavor, then this one is for you!

Yields: ½ gallon (2 quarts)

Ingredients:

2 heads Napa cabbage
½ cup sea salt
1 tablespoon fish sauce
5 green onions, chopped
½ small white onion, minced
2 cloves garlic, pressed
2 tablespoons white sugar
1 teaspoon ground ginger
5 tablespoons Korean chile powder

Directions:

Chop cabbage into 2-inch pieces. Mix cabbage and salt in a large bowl. Pound with a wooden spoon or cabbage crusher to release juices. Let sit for 5 minutes. Then pound again. These juices will replace water for a traditional fermentation.

Add remaining ingredients to mixture.

Pack mixture into a clean, quart jar. Weigh down vegetables so they are submerged in the brine with a fermentation weight or a plate that is just the right size. If there is not enough brine from the vegetable juices, add filtered water until is is 1-2 inches over vegetables.

Seal with an air-lock lid or an airtight lid. Air-tight lid will need to be cracked open daily to allow the carbon dioxide to escape.

Set in a cool, dark place for 3-6 days.

It will expanded and bubble. Periodically check it. Push down the vegetables if they come up above the water. If mold appears on the top, scrape it off as soon as possible to prevent further spoiling (the fermentation will prevent a small amount of mold from being a problem).

Taste periodically to see if it is ready.

Once it has reached a desired flavor, place in the refrigerator. The fermentation process will continue, slowly, and your kimchi will age like wine. Store up to 8 months!

Apple & Kale Kimchi

Here's one more fermented recipe which is healthy and tasty! A favorite among many!

Yields: ½ gallon (2 quarts)

Ingredients:

1 head of cabbage
1 bunch of kale
1 beet
1 green apple
½ clove organic garlic
¼ cup chopped leeks
1 carrot
2 tbsp sea salt
filtered water

Directions:

Chop cabbage and kale into 2-inch pieces. Shred beet, apple and carrot. Chop other veggies into desired size. Mix all ingredients (except water) in a large bowl. Pound with a wooden spoon or cabbage crusher to release juices. Let sit for 5 minutes. Then pound again. These juices will replace water for a traditional fermentation.

Pack mixture into 2, clean, quart jars. Weigh down vegetables so they are submerged in the brine with a fermentation weight or a plate that is just the right size. If there is not enough brine from the vegetable juices, add filtered water until is is 1-2 inches over vegetables.

Seal with an air-lock lid or an airtight lid. Air-tight lid will need to be cracked open daily to allow the carbon dioxide to escape.

Set in a cool, dark place for 3-6 days.

It will expanded and bubble. Periodically check it. Push down the vegetables if they come up above the water. If mold appears on the top, scrape it off as soon as possible to prevent further spoiling (the fermentation will prevent a small amount of mold from being a problem).

Taste periodically to see if it is ready.

Once it has reached a desired flavor, place in the refrigerator. The fermentation process will continue, slowly, and your kimchi will age like wine. Store up to 8 months!

Radish & Cabbage Kimchi

This kimchi has quite a bit of ingredients… but it is worth it! It can be eaten with your meal or on its own. It is delicious either way!

Yields: 2 quarts

Ingredients:

1 napa cabbage (about 2 pounds)
½ cup sea salt
8 ounces daikon radish, peeled and cut into 2-inch matchsticks
4 medium scallions, ends trimmed, cut into 1-inch pieces (use all parts)
⅓ cup Korean red pepper powder
¼ cup fish sauce
¼ cup peeled and minced fresh ginger (from about a 2-ounce piece)
1 tablespoon minced garlic cloves (from 6 to 8 medium cloves)
2 teaspoons Korean salted shrimp, minced
Filtered water

Directions:

Chop cabbage 2-inch pieces. Mix with salt. Pound with a wooden spoon or cabbage crusher to release juices. Let sit for 5 minutes. Then pound again. These juices will replace water for a traditional fermentation.

Prepare other vegetables as indicated above. Mix all ingredients (except water) in a large bowl. Mix everything together.

Pack mixture into 2, clean, quart jars. Weigh down vegetables so they are submerged in the brine with a fermentation weight or a plate that is just the right size. If there is not enough brine from the vegetable juices, add filtered water until is is 1-2 inches over vegetables.

Seal with an air-lock lid or an airtight lid. Air-tight lid will need to be cracked open daily to allow the carbon dioxide to escape.

Set in a cool, dark place for 3-6 days.

It will expanded and bubble. Periodically check it. Push down the vegetables if they come up above the water. If mold appears on the top, scrape it off as soon as possible to prevent further spoiling (the fermentation will prevent a small amount of mold from being a problem).

Taste periodically to see if it is ready.

Once it has reached a desired flavor, place in the refrigerator. The fermentation process will continue, slowly, and your kimchi will age like wine. Store up to 1 month!

Hot Radish Kimchi

If you love some heat to your food… than this recipe is just for you! The kick of the radish, paired with pepper flakes is delicious.

Yields: about 2 quarts

Ingredients:

4 pounds daikon radish, cut into 1" pieces.
¼ cup fish sauce
2 tbsp garlic, minced
1 tsp ginger, minced
5 stalks green onion chopped
⅔ cup hot pepper flakes
4 pounds of Korean radish
2 tbsp salt
2 tbsp sugar

Directions:

Chop radish. Mix with salt and sugar. Pound with a wooden spoon or cabbage crusher to release juices. Let sit for 20 minutes. Then pound again. Drain juice.

Prepare other vegetables as indicated above. Mix all ingredients in a large bowl.

Pack mixture into 2, clean, quart jars. Pour radish juice into jar so that it covers the mixture.

Weigh down vegetables so they are submerged in the brine with a fermentation weight or a plate that is just the right size. If there is not enough brine from the radish juices, add filtered water until is is 1-2 inches over vegetables.

Seal with an air-lock lid or an airtight lid. Air-tight lid will need to be cracked open daily to allow the carbon dioxide to escape.

Set in a cool, dark place for 3-6 days.

It will expanded and bubble. Periodically check it. Push down the vegetables if they come up above the water. If mold appears on the top, scrape it off as soon as possible to prevent further spoiling (the fermentation will prevent a small amount of mold from being a problem).

Taste periodically to see if it is ready.

Once it has reached a desired flavor, place in the refrigerator. The fermentation process will continue, slowly, and your kimchi will age like wine. Store up to 1 month!

Quick Kimchi

This kimchi is so easy and quick to make. Best for busy people who love kimchi but can't afford to give it too much time.

Yields: about 2 quarts

Ingredients:

2 pounds of cabbage
⅓ cup hot pepper flakes,
1 tbsp. sugar,
¼ cup kosher salt
¼ cup fish sauce,
¼ cup minced garlic,
3-4 stalks of chopped green onion (⅓ cup worth),
¼ cup's worth of julienned carrot

Directions:

Chop cabbage 2-inch pieces. Mix with salt and sugar. Pound with a wooden spoon or cabbage crusher to release juices. Let sit for 5 minutes. Then pound again. These juices will replace water for a traditional fermentation.

Prepare other vegetables as indicated above. Mix all ingredients in a large bowl.

Pack mixture into 2, clean, quart jars. Weigh down vegetables so they are submerged in the brine with a fermentation weight or a plate that is just the right size. If there is not enough brine from the vegetable juices, add filtered water until is is 1-2 inches over vegetables.

Seal with an air-lock lid or an airtight lid. Air-tight lid will need to be cracked open daily to allow the carbon dioxide to escape.

Good news! You can enjoy this right away!

But, if you prefer the taste of a longer ferment, set in a cool, dark place for 3-6 days.

It will expanded and bubble. Periodically check it. Push down the vegetables if they come up above the water. If mold appears on the top, scrape it off as soon as possible to prevent further spoiling (the fermentation will prevent a small amount of mold from being a problem).

Taste periodically to see if it is ready.

Once it has reached a desired flavor, place in the refrigerator. The fermentation process will continue, slowly, and your kimchi will age like wine. Store up to 1 month!

Individual Vegetables

The perfect snack! These veggies will be devoured in your home.

Fermented Carrot Sticks

Let's enjoy some carrots which are good for vision and when fermented they provide us probiotics too!

Yields: 1 quart mason jar

Ingredients:

1 – 1 ½ pounds of fresh carrots, trimmed
3 garlic cloves, peeled
2 cups filtered water
2 tablespoons of sea salt
one hefty outer cabbage leaf

Directions:

Dissolve salt in water (you may need to heat the water a bit to allow salt to dissolve. If so, bring water back to room temperature before moving forward).

Cut carrots into quarters, lengthwise. You will want them to be about 1.5 inches less than the height of your jar.

Place garlic cloves in the jar. Then, place carrot sticks vertically in jar. Pack them in so they are snug, but not over-packed.

Pour the brine over the carrot sticks so that they are completely covered. Leave 1" of space between the brine and the lip of the jar. Add more water, if needed.

Place the hefty outer cabbage leaf over the carrot sticks and tuck it into the sides as tightly between the carrots and the jar as you can. This will keep your carrots submerged and prevent rotting.

Seal with an air-lock lid or an airtight lid. An air-tight lid will need to be cracked open (then resealed) daily to allow the carbon dioxide to escape.

Set in a cool, dark place for 7-10 days.

It will expanded and bubble. Periodically check it as mentioned above. Push down the vegetables if they come up above the water. If mold appears on the top, scrape it off as soon as possible to prevent further spoiling (the fermentation will prevent a small amount of mold from being a problem).

After 7-10 days (it is safe to taste it to see if it is ready!), place in the refrigerator. The fermentation process will continue, slowly, and your carrots will age like wine. Store up to 8 months!

Fermented Ginger Carrots

This is super easy to make and tastes so delicious. Enjoy these carrots as a side dish with a burger or with your favorite salad!

Yields: about 1 quart

Ingredients:

4 cups finely shredded carrots
2 tablespoons fresh ginger, finely grated
2 tablespoon sea salt

Directions:

Shred carrots. A food processor can be very helpful.

Mix with salt and ginger. Pound with a wooden spoon or cabbage crusher to release juices. Let sit for 5 minutes. Then pound again. These juices will replace water for a traditional fermentation.

Place in jar. If needed, add filtered water to cover carrots. Weigh down vegetables so they are submerged in the brine with a fermentation weight or a plate that is just the right size. If there is not enough brine from the vegetable juices, add filtered water until is is 1-2 inches over vegetables.

Seal with an air-lock lid or an airtight lid. An air-tight lid will need to be cracked open (then resealed) daily to allow the carbon dioxide to escape.

Set in a cool, dark place for 7-10 days.

It will expanded and bubble. Periodically check it as mentioned above. Push down the vegetables if they come up above the water. If mold appears on the top, scrape it off as soon as possible to prevent further spoiling (the fermentation will prevent a small amount of mold from being a problem).

After 7-10 days (it is safe to taste it to see if it is ready!), place in the refrigerator. The fermentation process will continue, slowly, and your carrots will age like wine. Store up to 8 months!

Fermented Radishes

Radishes are commonly used in salads but besides that they flourish when fermented, giving you a delicious cultured vegetable recipe

Yields: 2, 1 quart jars

Ingredients:

4 cups filtered water
2 to 3 tablespoons sea salt
2 bunches of radishes, cut into quarters.
Optional seasoning seeds such as dill, mustard, caraway, etc.

Directions:

Dissolve salt in water (you may need to heat the water a bit to allow salt to dissolve. If so, bring water back to room temperature before moving forward). Add optional seasonings.

Prepare radishes as mentioned above.

Place radishes in jar. Pack them in so they are snug, but not over-packed.

Pour the brine over the radishes so that they are completely covered. Leave 1" of space between the brine and the lip of the jar. Add more water, if needed.

Weigh down vegetables so they are submerged in the brine with a fermentation weight or a plate that is just the right size. If there is not enough brine, add more filtered water until is is 1-2 inches over vegetables.

Seal with an air-lock lid or an airtight lid. An air-tight lid will need to be cracked open (then resealed) daily to allow the carbon dioxide to escape.

Set in a cool, dark place for 2-3 days.

It will expanded and bubble. Periodically check it as mentioned above. Push down the vegetables if they come up above the water. If mold appears on the top, scrape it off as soon as possible to prevent further spoiling (the fermentation will prevent a small amount of mold from being a problem).

After 2-3 days (it is safe to taste it to see if it is ready!), place in the refrigerator. The fermentation process will continue, slowly, and your radishes will age like wine. Store up to 8 months!

Fermented Spinach

Fermented Spinach loses its bitterness and turns out to sweet and salty instead. The addition of lemon makes this a refreshing recipe!

Yields:1 quart

Ingredients:

Enough spinach to tightly fill a wide-mouth quart jar, rinsed lightly, stems removed (about 1.5 pounds)
5 cloves garlic, minced fine
2 teaspoons sea salt
1 cup filtered water
½ lemon with peel, thinly sliced

Directions:

Mix with salt and spinach. Pound with a wooden spoon or cabbage crusher to release
juices. Let sit for 20 minutes. Then pound again.

Begin packing handfuls of the spinach into your jar. Periodically add a slice of lemon, layering and pressing the lemons and the spinach into the jar.

Once the jar is filled, pour water in slowly, only adding enough to bring the liquid level up to 1 inch away from the mouth of the jar.

Seal with an air-lock lid or an airtight lid. An air-tight lid will need to be cracked open (then resealed) daily to allow the carbon dioxide to escape.

Set in a cool, dark place for 7-10 days.

It will expanded and bubble. Periodically check it as mentioned above. Push down the vegetables if they come up above the water. If mold appears on the top, scrape it off as soon as possible to prevent further spoiling (the fermentation will prevent a small amount of mold from being a problem).

After 7-10 days (it is safe to taste it to see if it is ready!), place in the refrigerator. The fermentation process will continue, slowly, and your spinach will age like wine. Store up to 8 months!

Spicy Fermented Spinach

Want to add some kick to your fermented spinach? I've got just the trick...

Yields: 2 quarts

Ingredients:
12 – 16 c chopped spinach, stemmed
3 tbsp. sea salt
4 – 6 cloves garlic, finely chopped
1 fresh chile pepper, stemmed and seeded
½ lemon, seeded if you like, and cut into wedges or slices

Directions:
Mix with salt and spinach. Pound with a wooden spoon or cabbage crusher to release
juices. Let sit for 20 minutes. Then pound again. Mix remaining ingredients.

Pack spinach into jars. If there is not enough liquid, add filtered water so it cover the spinach.

Seal with an air-lock lid or an airtight lid. An air-tight lid will need to be cracked open (then resealed) daily to allow the carbon dioxide to escape.

Set in a cool, dark place for 7-10 days.

It will expanded and bubble. Periodically check it as mentioned above. Push down the vegetables if they come up above the water. If mold appears on the top, scrape it off as soon as possible to prevent further spoiling (the fermentation will prevent a small amount of mold from being a problem).

After 7-10 days (it is safe to taste it to see if it is ready!), place in the refrigerator. The fermentation process will continue, slowly, and your spinach will age like wine. Store up to 8 months!

Fermented Eggplant

A salted eggplant helps in removing its bitterness, but when fermented for days, they become more tasty and yummy!

Yields: 2 quarts

Ingredients:

2 medium eggplants, cut into long strips.
6 garlic cloves, smashed and peeled
2 teaspoons chopped fresh oregano
2 tablespoons chopped fresh basil
1 teaspoon red pepper flakes
2 tablespoons sea salt, plus more for salting eggplant
1 hefty outer cabbage leaf
1 quart water

Directions:

Sprinkle salt on egg plant. Let sit for 1-2 hours.

Dissolve salt in water (you may need to heat the water a bit to allow salt to dissolve. If so, bring water back to room temperature before moving forward).

Place garlic, red pepper flakes, and herbs in 2, 1-quart jars. Place eggplant strips vertical in jar. Once the jar is filled, pour brine in slowly, only adding enough to bring the liquid level up to 1 inch away from the mouth of the jar.

Place the hefty outer cabbage leaf over the eggplant sticks and tuck it into the sides as tightly between the eggplant and the jar as you can. This will keep your eggplant submerged and prevent rotting.

Seal with an air-lock lid or an airtight lid. An air-tight lid will need to be cracked open (then resealed) daily to allow the carbon dioxide to escape.

Set in a cool, dark place for 3-7 days.

It will expanded and bubble. Periodically check it as mentioned above. Push down the vegetables if they come up above the water. If mold appears on the top, scrape it off as soon as possible to prevent further spoiling (the fermentation will prevent a small amount of mold from being a problem).

After 3-7 days (it is safe to taste it to see if it is ready!), place in the refrigerator. The fermentation process will continue, slowly, and your eggplant will age like wine. Store up to 8 months!

Fermented Sweet Potatoes

Take a break from smashed and baked sweet potatoes. Instead, enjoy them in a tangy, crunchy form!

Yields: 2 quarts

Ingredients:

5 pounds sweet potatoes, sliced very thinly
1½-inch piece of fresh ginger, peeled and grated
1 large onion, diced
1 teaspoon cayenne powder
3-4 tablespoons sea salt

Directions:

Mix with salt and sweet potatoes. Pound with a wooden spoon or cabbage crusher to release juices. Let sit for 20 minutes. Then pound again. These juices will be your fermentation liquid.

Add remaining ingredients.

Place all ingredients into jar. If needed, add a bit of filtered water to that potatoes are covered.

Seal with an air-lock lid or an airtight lid. An air-tight lid will need to be cracked open (then resealed) daily to allow the carbon dioxide to escape.

Set in a cool, dark place for 7-10 days.

It will expanded and bubble. Periodically check it as mentioned above. Push down the vegetables if they come up above the water. If mold appears on the top, scrape it off as soon as possible to prevent further spoiling (the fermentation will prevent a small amount of mold from being a problem).

After 7-10 days (it is safe to taste it to see if it is ready!), place in the refrigerator. The fermentation process will continue, slowly, and your sweet potatoes will age like wine. Store up to 8 months!

Fermented Beets

Let's enjoy healthy beets in fermented form. A quick recipe which really looks good and is worth fermenting.

Yields: 1 quart

Ingredients:

9 medium beets, chopped into thin strips or shredded
2 tablespoon sea salt
1 cup filtered water

Directions:

Mix with salt and beets. Let sit for 20 minutes.

Place all ingredients into jar. If needed, add more filtered water to that beets are covered.

Seal with an air-lock lid or an airtight lid. An air-tight lid will need to be cracked open (then resealed) daily to allow the carbon dioxide to escape.

Set in a cool, dark place for 7-10 days.

It will expanded and bubble. Periodically check it as mentioned above. Push down the vegetables if they come up above the water. If mold appears on the top, scrape it off as soon as possible to prevent further spoiling (the fermentation will prevent a small amount of mold from being a problem).

After 7-10 days (it is safe to taste it to see if it is ready!), place in the refrigerator. The fermentation process will continue, slowly, and your beets will age like wine. Store up to 8 months!

Fermented Cucumbers

Do you love pickles? These fermented cucumbers will taste similar but have the benefits of probiotics that truly pickled foods do not have.

Yields: 1 quart

Ingredients:

3 cucumbers
1 tablespoon of fresh dill (optional)
2 tablespoon sea salt
1 cup of filtered water
hefty outer cabbage leaf

Directions:

Cut cucumbers into long, vertical strips.

Place vertical in jar.Add all other ingredients and shake to mix. If cucumbers are not covered, add more water.

Place the hefty outer cabbage leaf over the cucumber sticks and tuck it into the sides as tightly between the cucumber and the jar as you can. This will keep your cucumber submerged and prevent rotting.

Seal with an air-lock lid or an airtight lid. An air-tight lid will need to be cracked open (then resealed) daily to allow the carbon dioxide to escape.

Set in a cool, dark place for 3-5 days.

It will expanded and bubble. Periodically check it as mentioned above. Push down the vegetables if they come up above the water. If mold appears on the top, scrape it off as soon as possible to prevent further spoiling (the fermentation will prevent a small amount of mold from being a problem).

After 3-5 days (it is safe to taste it to see if it is ready!), place in the refrigerator. The fermentation process will continue, slowly, and your cucumber will age like wine. Store up to 8 months!

Fermented Spicy Radish Spears

If you were a fan of the chopped radishes above… than you will love these radish spears because they can be eaten with your hands!

Yields: 3 pints

Ingredients:

1 pound radishes cut into spears (approx ½" thick x 3" long)
2 tbsp. sea salt
2 cups filtered water
2 tbsp. Red pepper flakes
3 hefty cabbage leaves

Directions:

Cut radishes as mentioned above.

Dissolve salt in water (you may need to heat the water a bit to allow salt to dissolve. If so, bring water back to room temperature before moving forward). Add red pepper flakes. This is your brine.

Divide radishes into jars. Place strips vertical in jar. Once the jar is filled, pour brine in slowly, only adding enough to bring the liquid level up to 1 inch away from the mouth of the jars.

Place the hefty outer cabbage leaf over the radishes and tuck it into the sides as tightly between the vegetables and the jar as you can. This will keep your vegetables submerged and prevent rotting.

Seal with an air-lock lid or an airtight lid. An air-tight lid will need to be cracked open (then resealed) daily to allow the carbon dioxide to escape.

Set in a cool, dark place for 3-7 days.

It will expanded and bubble. Periodically check it as mentioned above. Push down the vegetables if they come up above the water. If mold appears on the top, scrape it off as soon as possible to prevent further spoiling (the fermentation will prevent a small amount of mold from being a problem).

After 3-7 days (it is safe to taste it to see if it is ready!), place in the refrigerator. The fermentation process will continue, slowly, and your radishes will age like wine. Store up to 8 months!

Fermented Green Beans

These fermented green beans are a great snack with a garlicky taste. They are so tasty, you'll just want to have more and more.

Yields: 1 quart

Ingredients:

¾ to 1 pound fresh green beans
1 large clove garlic, thinly sliced
pinch red pepper flakes
1 teaspoon dried dill OR 3 to 4 sprigs fresh dill
1½ Tablespoons unrefined sea salt
2 cups filtered water
hefty outer cabbage leaf

Directions:

Dissolve salt in water (you may need to heat the water a bit to allow salt to dissolve. If so, bring water back to room temperature before moving forward). This is your brine.

Snap off the stem-end of green beans. Place in boiling water for 2 minutes and immediately transfer to a bowl of ice water. Drain well and pat dry.

Place half of the sliced garlic into jar, followed by the red pepper flakes and dill.

Add green beans vertically in jar. Once the jar is filled, pour brine in slowly, only adding enough to bring the liquid level up to 1 inch away from the mouth of the jars. Sprinkle remaining garlic slices on top of beans in jar.

Place the hefty outer cabbage leaf over the green beans and tuck it into the sides as tightly between the vegetables and the jar as you can. This will keep your vegetables submerged and prevent rotting.

Seal with an air-lock lid or an airtight lid. An air-tight lid will need to be cracked open (then resealed) daily to allow the carbon dioxide to escape.

Set in a cool, dark place for 3-7 days.

It will expanded and bubble. Periodically check it as mentioned above.

After 3-7 days (it is safe to taste it to see if it is ready!), place in the refrigerator. The fermentation process will continue, slowly, and your green beans will age like wine. Store up to 8 months!

Curried Fermented Cauliflower

Cauliflower made tasty with delicious curry powder. Get ready for a fresh, crunchy and delicious taste.

Yields: 1 quart

Ingredients:

1 small head of cauliflower (about 3 cups of small florets), cut into pieces.
2½ tablespoons curry powder
4 cloves of garlic, smashed and peeled
3 tablespoons sea salt
1 quart of water
hefty outer cabbage leaf

Directions:

Dissolve salt in water (you may need to heat the water a bit to allow salt to dissolve. If so, bring water back to room temperature before moving forward). Add curry. This is your brine.

Place garlic in bottom of jar. Add cut cauliflower next. Once the jar is filled, pour brine in slowly, only adding enough to bring the liquid level up to 1 inch away from the mouth of the jars.

Place the hefty outer cabbage leaf over the cauliflower and tuck it into the sides as tightly between the vegetables and the jar as you can. This will keep your vegetables submerged and prevent rotting.

Seal with an air-lock lid or an airtight lid. An air-tight lid will need to be cracked open (then resealed) daily to allow the carbon dioxide to escape.

Set in a cool, dark place for 3-7 days.

It will expanded and bubble. Periodically check it as mentioned above.

After 3-7 days (it is safe to taste it to see if it is ready!), place in the refrigerator. The fermentation process will continue, slowly, and your cauliflower will age like wine. Store up to 8 months!

Fermented Dill Cauliflower

Cauliflowers are almost everyone's favorite but they become even more tasty and spicy with this fermentation recipe!

Yields: 1 quart

Ingredients:

3 cups cauliflower, cut into chunks
1 large garlic clove, crushed
1 tablespoon dry dill
3-4 peppercorns
1 bay leaf
2 tablespoons sea salt
2-3 cups filtered water
hefty outer cabbage leaf

Directions:

Dissolve salt in water (you may need to heat the water a bit to allow salt to dissolve. If so, bring water back to room temperature before moving forward). Add dill. This is your brine.

Place the bay leaf, garlic and peppercorns in bottom of jar. Add cut cauliflower next. Once the jar is filled, pour brine in slowly, only adding enough to bring the liquid level up to 1 inch away from the mouth of the jars.

Weigh down vegetables so they are submerged in the brine with a fermentation weight or a plate that is just the right size.

Seal with an air-lock lid or an airtight lid. An air-tight lid will need to be cracked open (then resealed) daily to allow the carbon dioxide to escape.

Set in a cool, dark place for 3-7 days.

It will expanded and bubble. Periodically check it as mentioned above.

After 3-7 days (it is safe to taste it to see if it is ready!), place in the refrigerator. The fermentation process will continue, slowly, and your cauliflower will age like wine. Store up to 8 months!

Polish Fermented Mushrooms

Have you ever fermented mushrooms? This unique recipe will be quite a treat. Here's how it is done!

Yields: 2 pints

Ingredients:

3 to 4 pounds fresh mushrooms, cleaned and stems removed
3 tbsp sea salt
6 to 10 juniper berries, crushed (optional)
1 teaspoon dried dill, or 2 tablespoons fresh
1 teaspoon caraway seed
2 teaspoons cracked black pepper
2 garlic cloves, smashed
hefty outer cabbage leaf

Directions:

Boil the mushrooms in lightly salted water for 5 minutes. Drain and let them cool in one layer on a paper towel or tea towel.

Dissolve salt in water (you may need to heat the water a bit to allow salt to dissolve. If so, bring water back to room temperature before moving forward). Add other spices. This is your brine.

Mushrooms into jars. Once the jar is filled, pour brine in slowly, only adding enough to bring the liquid level up to 1 inch away from the mouth of the jars.

Place the hefty outer cabbage leaf over the mushrooms and tuck it into the sides as tightly between the vegetables and the jar as you can. This will keep your vegetables submerged and prevent rotting.

Seal with an air-lock lid or an airtight lid. An air-tight lid will need to be cracked open (then resealed) daily to allow the carbon dioxide to escape.

Set in a cool, dark place for 3-7 days.

It will expanded and bubble. Periodically check it as mentioned above.

After 3-7 days (it is safe to taste it to see if it is ready!), place in the refrigerator. The fermentation process will continue, slowly, and your mushrooms will age like wine. Store up to 8 months!

Fermented Turnips

Turnips serve as a nutritious alternative to potatoes. If fermented, they become a crunchy, tangy, and delicious pickle for snacking.

Yields: 2 quarts

Ingredients:

12 medium turnips, scrubbed well and sliced 1/8 inch thick
2 teaspoons red pepper flakes
6 cups water
3-½ tablespoons sea salt
hefty outer cabbage leaf

Directions:

Dissolve salt in water (you may need to heat the water a bit to allow salt to dissolve. If so, bring water back to room temperature before moving forward). Add pepper flakes.

Place turnips in jar. Pour brine in slowly, only adding enough to bring the liquid level up to 1 inch away from the mouth of the jars.

Place the hefty outer cabbage leaf over the turnips and tuck it into the sides as tightly between the vegetables and the jar as you can. This will keep your vegetables submerged and prevent rotting.

Seal with an air-lock lid or an airtight lid. An air-tight lid will need to be cracked open (then resealed) daily to allow the carbon dioxide to escape.

Set in a cool, dark place for 3-7 days.

It will expanded and bubble. Periodically check it as mentioned above.

After 3-7 days (it is safe to taste it to see if it is ready!), place in the refrigerator. The fermentation process will continue, slowly, and your turnips will age like wine. Store up to 8 months!

Fermented Sweet Potatoes

Enjoy the richness of sweet potatoes for months by fermenting them with sea salt and coconut yogurt. The creaminess of this delicious treat makes is even suitable for dessert!

Yields: 2 cups

Ingredients:

2 large sweet potatoes, cut into large chunks
1 tablespoon sea salt
4 tablespoons coconut yogurt

Directions:

Bake chopped sweet potatoes in 350ºF oven for 45 minutes.

Mash with salt. Blend in yogurt.

Seal with an air-lock lid or an airtight lid. An air-tight lid will need to be cracked open (then resealed) daily to allow the carbon dioxide to escape.

Set in a cool, dark place for 3-7 days.

It will expanded and bubble. Periodically check it as mentioned above.

After 3-7 days (it is safe to taste it to see if it is ready!), place in the refrigerator. The fermentation process will continue, slowly, and your sweet potatoes will age like wine.

Fermented Cherry Tomatoes

These tangy and delicious cherry tomatoes are quick to make and incredibly refreshing.

Yields: 1 quart

Ingredients:

1 quart cherry tomatoes (number varies by size)
fresh basil leaves
2 cups filtered water
1.5 tbsp sea salt
1 large hefty cabbage leaf.

Directions:

Dissolve salt in water (you may need to heat the water a bit to allow salt to dissolve. If so, bring water back to room temperature before moving forward).

Place cherries and basil in jar. Pour brine in slowly, only adding enough to bring the liquid level up to 1 inch away from the mouth of the jar.

Place the hefty outer cabbage leaf over the cherries and tuck it into the sides as tightly between the vegetables and the jar as you can. This will keep your vegetables submerged and prevent rotting.

Seal with an air-lock lid or an airtight lid. An air-tight lid will need to be cracked open (then resealed) daily to allow the carbon dioxide to escape.

Set in a cool, dark place for 3-7 days.

It will expanded and bubble. Periodically check it as mentioned above.

After 3-7 days (it is safe to taste it to see if it is ready!), place in the refrigerator. The fermentation process will continue, slowly, and your tomatoes will age like wine. Store up to 8 months!

Fermented Green Cherry Tomatoes

Here is a tangy treat that is delicious without sacrificing the probiotic benefits of fermented vegetables. This recipe has quite a bit of ingredients but the preparation is completely worth it!

Yields: 1 quart

Ingredients:

4 cups small, whole green cherry tomatoes
½ cup sliced onion
4 cloves garlic, peeled
2 bay leaves
3 sprigs fresh dill leaves OR 1 teaspoon dried dill weed
1 teaspoon whole mustard seeds
½ teaspoon celery seed
4 whole allspice
4 black peppercorns
1 - 2 small hot chile peppers (optional)
4 cups filtered water
1 hefty outer cabbage leaf

Directions:

Dissolve salt in water (you may need to heat the water a bit to allow salt to dissolve. If so, bring water back to room temperature before moving forward). Add pepper flakes.

Place tomatoes in jar. Adding the onion, bay leaf, dill, mustard and celery seeds, allspice, black pepper and Chile peppers . Pour brine in slowly, only adding enough to bring the liquid level up to 1 inch away from the mouth of the jars.

Place the hefty outer cabbage leaf over the tomatoes and tuck it into the sides as tightly between the vegetables and the jar as you can. This will keep your vegetables submerged and prevent rotting.

Seal with an air-lock lid or an airtight lid. An air-tight lid will need to be cracked open (then resealed) daily to allow the carbon dioxide to escape.

Set in a cool, dark place for 5-7 days.

It will expanded and bubble. Periodically check it as mentioned above.

After 5-7 days (it is safe to taste it to see if it is ready!), place in the refrigerator. The fermentation process will continue, slowly, and your tomatoes will age like wine.

Fermented Horseradish Root

Did you know horseradish came from a root? Once you find the root at your local grocery store, you'll be addicted to making your own condiment!

Yields: About 1 cup

Ingredients:

about 1 cup fresh horseradish root (peeled and chopped)
1.5 tbsp unrefined sea salt
2 tbsp to ¼ cup filtered water

Directions:

Mix chopped horseradish root and sea salt in a food processor for about 1 minute. Add enough filtered water to make a smooth paste.

Spoon the mixture into a small jar, adding additional water to completely reach the top of the jar.

Seal with an air-lock lid or an airtight lid. An air-tight lid will need to be cracked open (then resealed) daily to allow the carbon dioxide to escape.

Set in a cool, dark place for 3-5 days.

It will expanded and bubble. Periodically check it as mentioned above.

After 3-5 days (it is safe to taste it to see if it is ready!), place in the refrigerator. The fermentation process will continue, slowly, and your horseradish will age like wine.

Fermented Chickpeas (Hummus)

Try this new twist on your traditional hummus. It will taste just as delicious and last much longer!

Yields: 2 cups

Ingredients:

16 ounces garbanzo beans (cooked)
3 cloves fermented garlic
1 Teaspoon sea salt
6 Tablespoon olive oil
4 Tablespoon lemon juice
2-3 Tablespoon tahini raw
1 Teaspoon cumin
1 Teaspoon hot curry (optional)
1 Teaspoon red pepper flakes (optional)

Directions:

Place all ingredients (except salt and tahini paste) in a food processor. Puree.

Add tahini and salt and mix by hand. If mixture is too thick, add more olive oil.

Seal with an air-lock lid or an airtight lid. An air-tight lid will need to be cracked open (then resealed) daily to allow the carbon dioxide to escape.

Set in the refrigerator. The fermentation process will continue, slowly, and your hummus will age like wine.

Mixed Vegetables

It's time to put all we have learned together and make some mixed veggie combos. This is the best of both worlds… you get veggies with the health benefits of all the previous recipes, but a variety to keep you craving these treats for months!

Fermented Cauliflower, Carrots, & Peppers

A delicious treat for cauliflower lovers. The jar looks so beautiful it can make for a great gift, too!

Yields: 2 quarts

Ingredients:

3 tablespoons sea salt
1 quart filtered water
1 cup small cauliflower florets
1 cup carrot chunks or slices
1 cup red bell pepper chunks or slices
1 clove garlic, smashed and peeled
1 bay leaf
½ teaspoon coriander seeds
¼ teaspoon black peppercorns
1 large hefty cabbage leaf

Directions:

Dissolve salt in water (you may need to heat the water a bit to allow salt to dissolve. If so, bring water back to room temperature before moving forward).

All other ingredients into jar. Pour brine in slowly, only adding enough to bring the liquid level up to 1 inch away from the mouth of the jars.

Place the hefty outer cabbage leaf over the veggies and tuck it into the sides as tightly between the vegetables and the jar as you can. This will keep your vegetables submerged and prevent rotting.

Seal with an air-lock lid or an airtight lid. An air-tight lid will need to be cracked open (then resealed) daily to allow the carbon dioxide to escape.

Set in a cool, dark place for 5-7 days.

It will expanded and bubble. Periodically check it as mentioned above.

After 5-7 days (it is safe to taste it to see if it is ready!), place in the refrigerator. The fermentation process will continue, slowly, and your veggies will age like wine.

Fermented Cauliflower, Carrots, and Garlic

Wow! What a combination. The garlic makes this one of my all-time favorites!

Yields: 1 quart

Ingredients:

3 garlic cloves, peeled and slightly crushed
3 cups cauliflower florets, rinsed in cold water
3 large carrots, cut into thin sticks
2 tablespoons sea salt
1 quart filtered water
1 hefty outer cabbage leaf

Directions:

Place the crushed garlic in the bottom of a clean quart jar. Then, layer cauliflower and carrots.

Dissolve salt in water (you may need to heat the water a bit to allow salt to dissolve. If so, bring water back to room temperature before moving forward).

Pour brine slowly into jar, only adding enough to bring the liquid level up to 1 inch away from the mouth of the jars.

Place the hefty outer cabbage leaf over the veggies and tuck it into the sides as tightly between the vegetables and the jar as you can. This will keep your vegetables submerged and prevent rotting.

Seal with an air-lock lid or an airtight lid. An air-tight lid will need to be cracked open (then resealed) daily to allow the carbon dioxide to escape.

Set in a cool, dark place for 5-7 days.

It will expanded and bubble. Periodically check it as mentioned above.

After 5-7 days (it is safe to taste it to see if it is ready!), place in the refrigerator. The fermentation process will continue, slowly, and your veggies will age like wine.

Fermented Beets and Turnips

This cold-weather root vegetable makes a classic combination to our winter meal and provides us much needed enzymes and probiotics.

Yields: 1 quart

Ingredients:

2 cups turnips washed, quartered, and sliced
1¼ cups beets washed, quartered, and sliced
2 tablespoons salt
2 Filtered water
1 hefty outer cabbage leaf

Directions:

Layer turnips and beets in jar.

Dissolve salt in water (you may need to heat the water a bit to allow salt to dissolve. If so, bring water back to room temperature before moving forward).

Pour brine slowly into jar, only adding enough to bring the liquid level up to 1 inch away from the mouth of the jars.

Place the hefty outer cabbage leaf over the veggies and tuck it into the sides as tightly between the vegetables and the jar as you can. This will keep your vegetables submerged and prevent rotting.

Seal with an air-lock lid or an airtight lid. An air-tight lid will need to be cracked open (then resealed) daily to allow the carbon dioxide to escape.

Set in a cool, dark place for 5-7 days.

It will expanded and bubble. Periodically check it as mentioned above.

After 5-7 days (it is safe to taste it to see if it is ready!), place in the refrigerator. The fermentation process will continue, slowly, and your veggies will age like wine.

Fermented Green Beans & Carrots

Looking for veggies for dinner? A jar of this in your fridge will make that task simple… and yummy!

Yields: 1 quart

Ingredients:

3 garlic cloves, peeled and slightly crushed
3 cups green beans, rinsed
3 large carrots, cut into thin sticks
2 tablespoons sea salt
1 quart filtered water
1 hefty outer cabbage leaf

Directions:

Place the crushed garlic in the bottom of a clean quart jar. Then, layer green beans and carrots.

Dissolve salt in water (you may need to heat the water a bit to allow salt to dissolve. If so, bring water back to room temperature before moving forward).

Pour brine slowly into jar, only adding enough to bring the liquid level up to 1 inch away from the mouth of the jars.

Place the hefty outer cabbage leaf over the veggies and tuck it into the sides as tightly between the vegetables and the jar as you can. This will keep your vegetables submerged and prevent rotting.

Seal with an air-lock lid or an airtight lid. An air-tight lid will need to be cracked open (then resealed) daily to allow the carbon dioxide to escape.

Set in a cool, dark place for 5-7 days.

It will expanded and bubble. Periodically check it as mentioned above.

After 5-7 days (it is safe to taste it to see if it is ready!), place in the refrigerator. The fermentation process will continue, slowly, and your veggies will age like wine.

Fermented Green Beans & Mushrooms

If you are a mushroom lover, than you know you can never have enough mushroom recipes. Keep mushrooms readily available and healthy with this delicious recipe!

Yields: 2 quarts

Ingredients:

3 garlic cloves, peeled and slightly crushed
2 cups green beans, rinsed
2 cups mushrooms, rinsed
2 tablespoons sea salt
1 quart filtered water
1 hefty outer cabbage leaf

Directions:

Place the crushed garlic in the bottom of jar. Then, layer green beans and mushrooms.

Dissolve salt in water (you may need to heat the water a bit to allow salt to dissolve. If so, bring water back to room temperature before moving forward).

Pour brine slowly into jar, only adding enough to bring the liquid level up to 1 inch away from the mouth of the jars.

Place the hefty outer cabbage leaf over the veggies and tuck it into the sides as tightly between the vegetables and the jar as you can. This will keep your vegetables submerged and prevent rotting.

Seal with an air-lock lid or an airtight lid. An air-tight lid will need to be cracked open (then resealed) daily to allow the carbon dioxide to escape.

Set in a cool, dark place for 5-7 days.

It will expanded and bubble. Periodically check it as mentioned above.

After 5-7 days (it is safe to taste it to see if it is ready!), place in the refrigerator. The fermentation process will continue, slowly, and your veggies will age like wine.

So, how did it go?

Did you try a recipe? Did you try all 37 recipes? Either way - did you love it?

Hopefully, you have made delicious snacks, and became healthier at the same time. After feeling energized and refreshed, be sure to try more!

Plus, don't forget to get your free gift for even more exciting recipes.

By now, you have realized just how easy (and delicious) the fermentation can be. If you are feeling generous, maybe you have shared this plan with your pickling Friends… you know, so they can be amazed by your probiotics!

I would love to hear how your fermenting adventure went. Email me your successes, your struggles, your questions, and your ideas!

Thank you again for being awesome and buying this book!

Here's to you and your health adventures,

Jennifer Connor

More Delicious Books By Jennifer Connor

If you like what you see, check out my author page to find more great recipes.

You can also join our Facebook group to receive free recipes right in your News Feed!

Here are just a few of the great recipe books you can grab!

37 Cheesecake Recipes: Easy and Delicious Cheesecakes That Are Better Than Your Mother's

37 Dump Cake Recipes: Easy and Delicious Dump Cakes That Are Better Than Your Grandmother's.

37 Gift Jar Recipes: Desserts: Inexpensive, DIY gifts that will make you more popular than Santa.

37 Gift Jar Recipes: Soups: Inexpensive, DIY gifts that will make you more popular than Santa.

37 Jerky Recipes: Beef and Other Game Jerky Recipes That Are Better Than Your Uncle's.

37 DASH Diet Recipes: Lose Weight and Lower Your Blood Pressure So You Can Look and Feel Healthier Than "That Skinny Girl".

37 Mediterranean Diet Recipes: Delicious and Healthy Meals That Will Help You Live as Long as A Greek

Copyright 2014 by Stukkie Software, LLC- All rights reserved.

All rights Reserved. No part of this publication or the information in it may be quoted from or reproduced in any form by means such as printing, scanning, photocopying or otherwise without prior written permission of the copyright holder.

Disclaimer and Terms of Use: Effort has been made to ensure that the information in this book is accurate and complete, however, the author and the publisher do not warrant the accuracy of the information, text and graphics contained within the book due to the rapidly changing nature of science, research, known and unknown facts and internet. The Author and the publisher do not hold any responsibility for errors, omissions or contrary interpretation of the subject matter herein. This book is presented solely for motivational and informational purposes only.

Lightning Source UK Ltd.
Milton Keynes UK
UKOW06f1816230815

257405UK00008B/222/P